Collins
MUSIC

How to teach
Whole-class
Instrumental
lessons

50
INSPIRING IDEAS

Kay Charlton

William Collins' dream of knowledge for all began with the publication of his first book in 1819.
A self-educated mill worker, he not only enriched millions of lives, but also founded a flourishing publishing house. Today, staying true to this spirit, Collins books are packed with inspiration, innovation and practical expertise. They place you at the centre of a world of possibility and give you exactly what you need to explore it. Collins. Freedom to teach.

An imprint of HarperCollins*Publishers*
The News Building
1 London Bridge Street
London
SE1 9GF

www.collins.co.uk

British Library Cataloguing in Publication Data
A catalogue record for this publication is available from the British Library.

Author: Kay Charlton
Commissioning editor: Naomi Cook
Development editor: Em Wilson
Cover designer: Angela English
Internal designer: Ken Vail Graphic Design
Production controller: Lyndsey Rogers
Printed and bound by CPI Group (UK) Ltd,
Croydon CR0 4YY

Acknowledgements

Thanks to fellow musicians, tutors and pupils past and present who have inspired my practice. Particular thanks to Plumcroft Primary School, where I honed my craft. Thanks too, to Naomi Cook, Collins Music Publisher, and Em Wilson, development editor, who made this book a reality.

Table of contents

Introduction

Whole-class instrumental lessons are a national programme of group instrumental teaching that takes place in schools. It was originally known as 'Wider Opportunities' and has evolved from an announcement made by the government in 2000, that *"all pupils in primary schools who wish to will have the opportunity to learn a musical instrument."* Its delivery is an essential part of each music hub's* core roles as outlined in the *National Plan for Music Education* (2011) and it is usually taught in Key Stage 2 (KS2). This type of tuition exists in many forms across England and has various names, including WCIT and First Access, and in some places it is still fondly known as 'wider opps'. It is most commonly called WCET (Whole Class Ensemble Teaching) so that is how I will refer to it in this book.

After pilot programmes in 2002–2003, Ofsted recommended that *"over time, all pupils in Key Stage 2 should have access to a free trial period of specialist instrumental tuition, wherever possible lasting for at least one year"* (Ofsted, 2004), and that programmes should provide children with:

◗ New musical experiences.

◗ Acquisition of musical skills.

◗ Specialist instrumental tuition.

This is broadly the way lessons are delivered now; the length of time children receive instruction varies, as does the mode of delivery and the instrument learnt. A 2017 report (Fautley, Kinsella, and Whittaker) found more than 35 instruments were taught through WCET. This kind of group teaching is very different to the traditional one-to-one way of teaching, the way you may have learnt your instrument, and it can be challenging!

This book is a collection of ideas, including those gathered from musicians, fellow tutors and pupils I have taught over the years, and is designed to give you practical advice for planning your WCET lessons and developing your own philosophy of tuition – what you will teach and how you will teach it – whilst putting children at the centre of a rich musical experience. Good luck!

*"Music Education Hubs are groups of organisations – such as local authorities, schools, other hubs, art organisations, community or voluntary organisations – working together to deliver joined-up music education provision." **(artscouncil.org.uk/music-education/music-education-hubs#section-1)**

How to use this book

Dip into this book whenever you want a flash of inspiration to improve and inspire your whole-class instrumental teaching.

The ideas in this book are organised by theme – these are given at the foot of each page. Each idea follows a very simple format:

❍ **Title:** the catchy title sums up what the idea is about.

❍ **Quote:** the opening quote from a teacher or student captures the essence of the idea.

❍ **Overview:** the quick overview of the idea will help you select a new idea to read or re-find an idea you found useful on a previous flick-through.

❍ **Idea:** the idea itself.

❍ **Hints and tips:** additional teaching tips, suggestions for ways to take the idea further, anecdotes, checklists and bonus ideas are provided throughout.

Setting up your space 1

"Make the teaching space work for you."

The way you organise your teaching space can have a big impact on a lesson. Get it right early on and teaching and learning will be easier for all involved.

The space you are given may not be your ideal classroom; in fact it may not be a classroom at all. You could be teaching in the hall, in a corridor, in an open-plan space, in the 'music hut', even on the top deck of a double-decker bus in the playground! Schools are always short of space, so making the best of it may be the only way forward.

◗ Organise the space so that children are sitting away from tables with enough room to play and avoid guitars or bows from bumping into each other; a semicircle is ideal if there is space.

◗ If possible, establish a setting up routine with children helping to move chairs and set up the space.

◗ Make sure there are chairs or benches available to avoid fidgeting and complaining – children get tired if made to stand for long periods. By all means stand them up to play, but sit the group down while you are talking or demonstrating.

◗ Make sure you have eye contact with all children at all times.

◗ Vary where children sit so that they can't sit at the back every week.

◗ Ask the class teacher whether there are children who shouldn't be sitting together.

◗ Don't forget to leave the room as you found it.

Top tip

Make sure you can see everyone and make sure children know you can see them.

Anecdote

My school actually does have a red double-decker bus in the playground! It's often used for teaching groups and is the permanent home of the school drum kit.

2 Allocating instruments

"Learning how to take care of an instrument gives children a sense of pride and ownership."

Establish safe routines and rules from the beginning – opening cases carefully and holding instruments correctly and with good posture.

Children instinctively want the biggest case, the shiniest instrument, the red one…! Don't let children choose or grab an instrument, establish a system of distribution and stick to it.

◑ Instruments with cases: The first time you give instruments out, explain carefully how to open the case. This may take some time, but it will make life easier later on and ensure that instruments don't get dropped or damaged.

- Place the case on the floor, not on your lap. Make sure the handle is facing you and the case is the right way up.
- Explain how to open catches, clips or zips – **children won't know how to do this!**
- Leave the instrument in the case until you explain how to pick it up.

◑ Demonstrate how to pick up and hold the instrument: Whatever it is, you will need to establish a clear routine for this. These are my instructions for a trumpet:

> **Top tip**
>
> Establish a 'rest' position for when you need children to listen, e.g. sitting with instruments on their laps, hands away from strings and drum heads. This will avoid 'fiddling' and playing when they should be listening to you. Model this and children will copy you.

- While the trumpet is still in the case, carefully put in the mouthpiece.
- Put your left hand out in front of you; imagine you are holding a large glass of water in this hand.
- Pick up the trumpet with your other hand and transfer it into your left hand so your left hand is around the valve casing and the mouthpiece is facing you.
- Imagine you are holding a large glass of water in your right hand; tip it up as though to drink. Put this hand on top of the valves – one finger for each valve and your little finger round the hook.
- Demonstrate where to put the thumb.

Instgument maintenance 3

"Miss, my valve is stuck..."

Keeping on top of maintenance can mean the difference between a lesson going well and being disrupted by on-the-spot repairs.

Instruments need to be in good working order, with valves working and no broken reeds, strings or drum heads.

⊙ You are the specialist, you know what is needed. If repairs or replacements are required, ask your music hub or school – you can't teach efficiently if equipment isn't up to scratch.

⊙ Keep a good supply of reeds, strings, rosin, cleaning wipes and valve oil so that you don't run out.

⊙ If instruments do let you down, don't let it distract your focus – children get bored if a lesson goes off task for too long. If you have to fix something, keep children occupied with a specific exercise and clear instructions, e.g. all playing along with a backing track, individual practice or taking turns to lead the class in a group practice. Be prepared to multi-task: fix the problem whilst keeping an eye on proceedings.

⊙ Stringed instruments need to be tuned before each lesson and this will need to be built into your setting up time; you may be able to train up a member of school staff or a teaching assistant to help you. Make sure children don't touch tuning pegs in the lesson!

⊙ Hygiene is particularly important when teaching woodwind or brass instruments. There should be no sharing of instruments, mouthpieces or reeds. Teach the children how to clean their instrument after use.

> **Top tip**
>
> Make sure you follow the latest guidance on cleaning instruments.

4 Learning names

"It's really hard to teach children if you don't know who they are!"

Getting to know children by name is essential if you are to engage with them successfully. Here are some ideas for learning names musically whilst practising technique along the way.

If you don't know a child's name, it is impossible to keep a record of their ability and progress. Discipline is also difficult – calling a name quietly is a better way to get a child's attention than waving at them. The answer is to keep a register (first names only for safeguarding reasons, and always check with the school first). As well as recording attendance, every couple of weeks write a quick note on their progress.

Playing with names

As soon as children can produce a sound, get them to play their name rhythm – you may need to help them with the number of syllables in their name. They will need to use articulation to play the rhythm, which is a great way to introduce technique such as tonguing/plucking/bowing/strumming or a particular tone on the djembe. Remind children that you are learning their names, just as they are learning to play an instrument.

● Give children time to practise their name rhythm. Try using a drum track or play a groove on the drums or piano to introduce the concept of playing rhythmically to a pulse; encourage children to be inventive with their rhythm – how many different ways can they play their name using long and short notes? Can they play it differently each week?

Top tip

Many drum backing tracks are available online. My favourite is Jim Dooley. He has recorded drum loops and beats from swing to funk to rock at a range of tempi, see: **jimdooley.net.**

● Take the register and hear each name played back. This gives you the chance to hear progress, check on technique and give some quick individualised feedback.

● Keep the rest of the group engaged while you are doing this – what advice would they give to improve someone's sound? Can they keep the pulse with body percussion until it's their turn to play? Or, play a 'chorus' riff together between names.

Giving feedback 5

"Well done, now let's work on the dynamics..."

We all like to be praised for our work, but giving feedback in the right way is important and can affect the way a child feels about their learning.

Feedback should be appropriate, truthful, supportive and constructive – showing ways to improve.

● Don't say something is great if it isn't – a child will know it isn't great! An appropriate and useful comment could be: "Good try, that is getting better; don't forget to use this finger for F instead of that one."

● Ask the children what they think – how did it sound, how can it be improved? If children understand where they are going wrong, they are more likely to understand how to make progress.

● Try to give individuals feedback whenever possible. Keep a note of their progress (see Idea 11) so that you can praise improvement on specific aspects of their playing.

● Think about the language you are using – can you turn a negative into a positive? Consider the effect of the following phrases:

Top tip

Be specific. Be clear. Be constructive. Don't over-praise.

Negative	Positive
That didn't sound very good, let's do it again.	What a lovely sound some people are making, let's all aim for a lovely sound this time.
Your strumming pattern was wrong again.	Are we all together on this strumming pattern? Who can show us the right pattern?
Someone isn't playing the right notes.	Did that sound right? Were we all playing the same notes?
You've all forgotten what we did last week!	Shall we go over what we learnt last week? Who can start us off?

6 Pedagogy

"I hear the word 'pedagogy', but don't really know what it means."

Put simply, pedagogy (pronounced 'pe-da-go-jee') is how skills and knowledge are delivered – what you are teaching and how you are teaching it; the theory and practice of your teaching.

There are many pedagogical theories, and they have changed over the years. The traditional (you might say old-fashioned) style of teaching has been labelled 'behaviourism' – it was **teacher-centred** and based on direct instruction, with the teacher being 'right'. WCET lessons won't flourish with a behaviourist pedagogy.

The better approach is **child-centred**. It takes into account learners' backgrounds – their 'enculturation', and the way their existing knowledge interacts with instruction. Learners are actively involved in their learning rather than receiving information passively.

◉ Consider the context of each teaching situation and what delivery process is right for your children: What works in one-to-one or small-group lessons will work differently in a WCET group situation.

Taking it further...

If you want to read up on pedagogical theory or teaching methods, try these authors and bloggers who have written extensively on classroom and instrumental teaching:
- Paul Harris
- Martin Fautley
- John Finney
- Ally Daubney
- Susan Hallam
- Keith Swanwick
- Janet Mills
- Anita Holford
- Chris Philpott

◉ Who are you teaching and what are your long-term goals or learning outcomes for them? Don't forget that children's enculturation will affect the way they learn and their musical experiences will all be different. How can you build on their existing knowledge and prior learning?

◉ Planning should go hand-in-hand with assessment: Reflect on what learning has taken place in a lesson and plan your teaching strategy and next lesson content appropriately, each week building on children's learning.

◉ Keep children actively involved: Use open questioning and make sure everyone is engaged through activities that challenge children at an appropriate level.

◉ Embed musical skills through practice: Learn musical concepts such as dynamics through playing so that terminology is wedded to actions.

Building a WCET curriculum 7

"Understanding the National Curriculum for Music will help you to build your own ideas from a solid foundation."

The National Curriculum is a good place to start when planning your own WCET curriculum. It is a very quick read – only 127 words! This means it is open to interpretation, giving you the freedom to build a broad syllabus covering general musicianship and instrumental skills.

WCET is intended to support the delivery of the National Curriculum for Music in England, not replace it. However, school budgets, timetabling or lack of in-school expertise often means that WCET is the only music tuition provided for a year group. You therefore need to plan a broad musical WCET curriculum.

The key statements in the National Curriculum include phrases such as: *"sing and play musically with increasing confidence and control"* and *"play instruments with increasing accuracy, fluency and expression"*. They also include some more specific ideas:

○ Performing, listening and composing: These are the main strands of the Curriculum – a high quality, balanced programme should address all three.

○ Aural memory: Explore improvisation and learning by ear (see Ideas 22 and 27).

○ Solo and ensemble playing: Find opportunities to perform to others (see Idea 33).

○ Singing: Learn songs and use the voice for internalising (see Idea 21).

○ Inter-related dimensions: Explore playing with variety and expression (see Idea 8).

○ Genre: Listen to, play and sing music from a diverse range of traditions and styles (see Idea 23).

○ Notation: Include an introduction to *"staff and other musical notations"* (see Ideas 39–40).

The National Curriculum gives plenty of ideas for content; your job is to deliver sessions musically, creatively and inclusively, at an appropriate level for everyone.

Taking it further...

To find out more, read the National Curriculum at **gov.uk**.

8 The inter-related dimensions

"Pitch means high and low."

In the 2013 National Curriculum, the 'elements' of music were re-named as the 'inter-related dimensions'. Whatever we call them, these fundamental musical concepts are the building blocks of any piece of music.

Ensure that these concepts are learnt through playing or 'doing' and not as abstract words; knowing that 'pitch means high and low' is not the same as being able to recognise the difference between two pitches and being able to reproduce them on an instrument.

Here are some ideas for embedding these concepts in your teaching:

◐ Pulse: a steady beat (not a rhythm pattern) – Most music has a pulse. Listen to some recorded music, and practise feeling the pulse: march on the spot or tap parts of the body in time. Ask children to take turns to be the leader by choosing how the group maintains the pulse.

◐ Tempo: the speed of the music – Try playing or singing a piece at different speeds and ask children to describe how the music made them feel, e.g. relaxed, racing, etc. Play to the children, changing speed suddenly or gradually and ask children to respond to your changes with movements that reflect the feel of the music.

◐ Pitch: high and low notes – Play a series of notes on your instrument and ask children to stand/sit or raise/lower their hands in response to the changes in pitch. Then ask them to respond with their eyes shut!

◐ Dynamics: volume, e.g. loud (*forte*) and soft (*piano*) – Make sure children understand that dynamics are not the same as high and low (pitch), even though, confusingly, we say 'turn the volume up'. Teach the children that changes in dynamics can occur suddenly or gradually, e.g. demonstrate a *crescendo* by all tapping knees gently and gradually getting louder. Try it on instruments.

> **Top tip**
>
> Explore silence in music. A rest, or silent beat/s, can be very powerful in music, creating a sense of anticipation. Conduct the children playing a long note or phrase; when you stop them, they all freeze. Try a decrescendo that fades away to silence…

- **Timbre**: the sound of the instrument; the quality of the sound; tone colour – Listen to a piece of music and ask the children how the choice of instruments enhances the sound. I like to use Miles Davis's *A Kind of Blue* to demonstrate how the Harmon mute has a completely different sound to an un-muted trumpet and gives the music a particular atmosphere.
- **Structure**: how the music is constructed – Introduce structure as being like a sandwich; each filling is a different section, or theme, and you can have as many fillings as you like. Refer to real terminology, e.g. intro/outro, verse/chorus, the 'head' and 'solos' in jazz.
- **Duration**: long and short sounds that make up the rhythm of a piece – Draw lines and dashes on the board and practise playing some Morse code patterns. Try conducting long and short notes, e.g. a chopping signal for short sounds (one hand chopping into the palm of the other hand) and a horizontal moving hand for a long sound.
- **Texture**: layers of sound; the combination of different instruments; 'thick' or 'thin' – Listen to a piece of music that starts with a few instruments and moves to a thicker texture (e.g. Ravel's *Boléro*). Conduct texture with your group: start a few children playing, open your arms to encompass more players then gradually widen your arms to include the whole group. Invite children to be the leader.
- **Notation:** how music may be written down – The National Curriculum lists 'appropriate musical notations' with the inter-related dimensions of music, but I like to think of it separately. For a detailed look at notation, see Ideas 39–40.

Taking it further...

The *Musical Elements Song* illustrates the inter-related dimensions to the tune of *Twinkle, Twinkle Little Star*. Make up some actions to interpret the words. **teachingideas.co.uk/musical-elements/musical-elements-song**

9 Planning

"What shall we do this week...?"

Planning for musical learning will ensure your lessons have structure and direction, and that children make progress and meet goals.

If your lesson has variety, pace and engaging content with a creative approach to resources, musical learning will take place and children should make progress. In order to achieve this, planning is essential. Where do you want children to be by the end of the year, or by the end of a term, or one lesson? How will you achieve your musical goals? Be clear in your objectives – plan an overview of learning for each term then break it down into a half-term scheme, then a weekly plan.

Create a simple template for your long-term and medium-term planning, e.g.

Week	Termly overview			
	Objectives, repertoire and activities	Success criteria – outcomes		
		Working towards	Working at	Working beyond
1				
2				

A more detailed weekly plan will include: the lesson focus, repertoire/resources needed, lesson objectives, activities with timings.

Remember, once you have planned a year's lessons, you can use the plan again and again, adjusting and improving as you go.

Plan the structure of your lessons

● Make sure you start with music; teaching by demonstration and modelling is more effective than verbally explaining something!

● Do a warm-up that is relevant to the main part of the lesson.

● Demonstrate new ideas through your instrument – play rather than talk!

● Keeping children interested and engaged is key to a successful lesson – plan for more than one activity and don't spend too long doing one thing (see Idea 10).

● Reinforce musical knowledge and techniques but make sure there is always something new – have children made progress and moved on from last week?

● Plan your lesson so that it has a logical flow, building on prior learning – activities should gradually grow in complexity.

● Be prepared to recap things covered in the previous week's lesson – children may learn something one week and seem to have completely forgotten it by the next; it may not transfer from the short-term to the long-term memory without repeated reminders. As musicians we know the value of 'playing it in'.

Evaluate progress and reflect on the success of the lesson

● Reflect on the lesson – did it go to plan? Was there a good pace to activities? What would you do differently next time?

● What are the outcomes or success criteria – have the learning objectives been met?

● How do you know that children have learnt what you intended – what's the evidence?

● How will you assess children's success?

Your evaluation will affect your planning for the next lesson – did everything work as planned or did you have to adjust your plan?

(For more on assessment, see Idea 11.)

Checklist ✔

- Prepare resources in advance.
- Do a warm-up that is relevant to the main part of the lesson, focus on a key feature and aim for 80% playing and 20% speaking.
- Include opportunities to perform, compose, improvise and listen critically.
- Ensure that all children are involved and engaged at their level.
- Plan lessons that are musical and fun!

10 Pace – keep it snappy!

"A good lesson should have a variety of activities delivered at the right speed with a sense of flow."

Make sure your lesson flows from one activity to the next and that resources are ready so there are no delays which would give children time to become distracted. Changing the pace or inserting a musical game are both excellent ways to gain children's focus.

You don't want to move too fast – or too slow – so how long should you spend on each activity? This depends on your class and the timetabling of your lesson. Straight after lunch, after wet play or at the end of the week can be a challenging time! Don't overload children with too much information – deliver material in bite-sized, digestible chunks and change the focus between playing, singing and rhythm activities to keep up class energy.

Top tip

Ofsted includes pace as a key indicator of success: *"Each section [of the lesson] is built on the last and supports the next at a pace that continues to engage children throughout."* (Ofsted) This is good advice and is achieved through planning and preparation and knowing what your musical goals are and where your lesson is going.

Changing the pace of a lesson will stop children getting bored or restless and will keep them engaged and focused on learning. Here are some examples of ways to change the pace within a lesson:

○ Listening activity: Listen to a piece of music and ask children to talk to their neighbour and think of three words to describe the music they just heard.

○ Change position: e.g. "Let's stand up/sit down to play this time."

○ Break off and work in pairs: Ask children to work in pairs and have a musical conversation playing question and answer phrases on their instruments.

○ Time for individual practice: Take five minutes for children to practise playing the tune in their own time/improvise over a backing track/make up a tune using set notes.

○ Musical game: Take a break from the main learning to play a musical game.

A game is great for focusing/refocusing restless children. It's also a sneaky way of working on core musical skills (see Idea 35).

The number game: Practise internalising the pulse whilst engaging in a physical workout.

Stand up, without instruments. As a group and in time (count it in), tap heads while counting to eight out loud; then tap shoulders for eight, then knees, then toes. Without stopping, repeat the routine – counting to four, then two then one on head, shoulders, knees, toes.

Discuss the activity, e.g. ask what the numbers are doing (halving). Ask whether you were all together at the end. If not, why – what happened? (Usually the group speeds up – particularly on the knees, which is the loudest part!)

Explain that the objective is to keep together; remind children of the musical concepts of pulse and tempo. You could add a clap or an action (in time) at the end after the 'ones' to prove that the class is together.

Try again (without speeding up!).

Try repeating the game at a faster tempo.

Then try it without counting out loud – counting in your head, or 'thinking voice'.

> **Bonus idea**
>
> Try the game with eyes closed! Inevitably, children will all finish at different times, proving that we rely on both looking and listening when making music together.

11 Assessment

"How did we do today?"

A good teacher is constantly making judgements; how can you use assessment to help children improve, make progress, and eventually move onto the next stage of instrumental learning?

Time is of the essence when teaching, so an efficient and quick way of assessing and recording progress and evidence of children's skills, knowledge and understanding is essential.

● Recording progress: Use a simple three-point scale; commonly two sets of wording are used interchangeably:

Working towards	Requires additional support
Working at	Making expected progress
Working beyond	Working at greater depth

These statements can be applied to various musical criteria, e.g. aural/copy-back skills; technical skills; creativity; tone; musical understanding.

● Progress spider diagrams: Progress can also be clearly evidenced on a spider diagram, with as many 'legs' as you like, e.g.

Bonus idea

Self-assessment and peer-assessment are important skills, which take practice; encourage children to do this constructively. For self-assessment, a simple thumbs up/medium/down can give you a quick overall impression of how individuals are feeling about a task.

Use the spider diagram to chart the progress of individual children or groups over time. At the end of each term put a dot on each leg to show each child's progress; the closer to the centre, the higher the achievement.

Don't assess too often; once a term will give a clear indication of progress. As well as being useful for school records and end of year reports, this evidence will inform your planning for each child, showing those who need more support and those who need to be pushed a little harder.

Differentiation 12

"Some children are struggling, what can I do?"

The children in your group will be mixed ability. They probably didn't choose their instrument; it may not be suitable for their physique or one that they feel an affinity for. So, how can we ensure that all children learn and make progress?

Differentiation means responding to individual needs: some children may struggle with certain musical concepts or find it difficult to produce a clear sound; others may already have some technique and musical knowledge; most will be somewhere in the middle. For lessons to be inclusive and accessible, some differentiation is essential.

○ Differentiation by task: Provide a simplified and/or more complex version of an activity, e.g.

Simplifying
- Play only on beat one of the melody but make sure it sounds great and is squarely on the beat.
- Play easier rhythm patterns, chords or notes, e.g. an ostinato, simple harmony, longer notes or bass line.
- Sing or clap instead of playing; play pizzicato instead of bowed.

Making it more complex
- Invite a child to play a section on their own as a solo.
- Play a more complicated strumming/rhythm pattern; play chords instead of single notes; add a harmony line; on the keyboard, play the melody with two hands.

○ Differentiation by learning style: Plan activities using various learning styles and with your help, allow children to choose the approach that fits them best.

Visual – a preference for images: seeing note names written down, using notation or a graphic representation of fingering.

Auditory – learning by ear, away from notation.

Kinaesthetic – physical learning: using the body, hands and sense of touch, feeling your way round the instrument and using your 'muscle memory'.

> **Top tip**
>
> Always plan for differentiation in your teaching.

13 Scaffolding learning

"How can I support learning in my group?"

A scaffold supports a structure until it is secure, it can then be taken away. Lessons should be planned to support learning, enabling children to achieve something that they couldn't do unassisted.

As part of planning for musical learning you will be aiming to pitch lessons at the right level for your group. If a task is too easy, children will get bored; if it's too hard they will switch off. So, plan activities with an appropriate level of challenge – one that is achievable with your support.

Essentially, scaffolding means showing your group how to play something through modelling, then supporting their learning of the new concept by teaching it in small steps – playing along with them until they are confident. Gradually, as children become more adept at the activity, you can leave them to play unaided. If your planned lesson is interactive, building on prior learning, then the task will be achievable and enjoyable with pleasing musical results.

Taking it further...

Once children can play a piece confidently, ask them to make musical choices and lead the music by:
- Deciding on the tempo.
- Counting the piece in.
- Conducting – starting/stopping the music.
- Shaping the dynamics.
- Changing the tempo – getting faster or slower.
- Taking solos.

Scaffolding learning

❍ Hear and/or see the new concept being played.

❍ Understand what to do in order to learn it.

❍ Sing it – make up words to remember the rhythm patterns or melody.

❍ Clap the pulse/rhythm away from the instrument.

❍ Sing the melody whilst practising the fingering or hand positions.

❍ Practise the fingering or positions without making a sound while the teacher plays.

❍ Have visual resources to refer to if needed.

❍ Play all together, slowly.

❍ Gradually increase the tempo.

❍ Eventually the group plays without the teacher's support.

Making instrumental 14
progress

"The first time I tried I couldn't make a sound, now I can play lots of notes."

What is the purpose of WCET – to teach general musicianship through an instrument, or purely to teach instrumental skills? This is a popular debate! In a group teaching situation the former is the best option, but don't forget the nuts and bolts of instrumental learning.

Most WCET programmes include the teaching of general musicianship, which underpins instrumental skills and contributes to a rich and musical learning experience. Technical progress on the instrument may be slow – children on melodic instruments may only learn 5–6 notes in a year – but creativity can take place as soon as we make a sound, putting in motion deep, vertical and broad musical progress; increasing technical fluency underpinned by general musicianship.

After a term, children should be able to play (or at least understand how to play) some clear consecutive notes, strum simple chords or play simple rhythm patterns, produced with correct technique and good posture. They should have the confidence and know-how to play a simple piece together and/or alone and to copy back patterns and make up a simple reply.

Where could your group be by the end of a year? Aim to produce confident players who are ready to move on to one-to-one lessons and/or join a progression ensemble (see Idea 46).

If you are an enthusiastic teacher with well-planned progressive activities, musical progress will be fun and goals will be achievable.

Checklist ✔

- Be realistic: it's better to play a simple piece well than a complicated one badly.
- Use different approaches and differentiated activities so that everyone is working to their strengths (see Idea 12).
- Be a reflective practitioner – how did the lesson go? Did all the activities work? Did all children make progress and achieve something in the lesson?

15 Children's musical development

"How do children learn...?"

Understanding children's physical and cognitive development will help you to understand how they learn and their capacity to make musical progress.

Young children are aware only of their senses and physical needs, but by the time you are likely to be teaching them in KS2, they are moving towards being able to use logic, to think, solve problems and to make connections. Identifying what kind, and what level of information children are capable of processing will help to inform your planning and assessment.

In terms of their musical development, you are reliant to some extent on what musical education they have had so far. Some schools will provide regular music lessons; in others, music may have been delivered only sporadically.

○ **Development by age:** The Swanwick–Tillman model (1986) attempted to categorise children's musical development:

Top tip

The sequence of learning is important, e.g. to walk before you run; to recognise sounds, then words then write. And, in music, to recognise and internalise musical sounds, durations and other musical knowledge before learning notation(s) – 'sound before symbol'.

4–5 years: Rambling exploration of the voice or instrument; an awareness of expression in music or moods and character in a musical passage. Children may easily relate music to a story, visual images or other external associations.

7–8 years: Able to use sound for expressive purposes. Children recognise established musical conventions and may be able to identify metre, repetitions and other musical features.

10–11 years: Able to recognise conventional structures (e.g. verse/chorus), and changes in musical concepts such as timbre, dynamics, tempo, pitch, rhythm.

◑ Development over time: The National Curriculum level descriptors (2010) are no longer in use, but this sample extract shows how the expectations of children's musical skills and understanding develop over time:

'Level 2' (c. 7 years old)   **'Level 3'** (c. 9 years old)

'Level 2' (c. 7 years old)		'Level 3' (c. 9 years old)
Recognise and explore how sounds can be organised.	⟶	Recognise and explore the ways sounds can be combined and used expressively.
Sing with a sense of the shape of the melody.	⟶	Sing in tune with expression and perform simple melodic and rhythmic parts.
Perform simple patterns and accompaniments keeping to a steady pulse.	⟶	Improvise repeated patterns and combine several layers of sound with an awareness of the combined effect.
Improve their own work.	⟶	Recognise how different musical elements are combined and used expressively and make improvements to their own work.

◑ Encouraging independent learning:
We learn more effectively when we understand *how* to learn. This is called 'metacognition'. As children's capacity develops, guide them towards becoming independent learners, e.g.

- Thinking for themselves.
- Being unafraid to take risks and try things out.
- Being aware of their own strengths and weaknesses.
- Understanding how to practise and what strategies are available to get better.
- Identifying problems and how to solve them.
- Knowing how to reflect on their work and evaluate it.
- Wanting to improve and understanding how to.

Taking it further...

Make sure activities are pitched at the appropriate level for children's development. Give children the tools they need to become independent learners, the space to try things out, to make their own musical decisions and conclusions and to make connections in their music-making (see Idea 32).

16 Knowledge and learning

"Consider these three types of musical knowledge: knowledge about, know-how and knowledge of."

Learning develops both knowledge and skills, and the way children learn depends on any number of factors, both intrinsic and extrinsic. In this idea, we think about that thing called 'learning' in music, and the importance of learning knowledge about, know-how and knowledge of.

We know learning has taken place when something has changed – children can play something new, or can explain how to play it. The rate of change, or learning, is influenced by many things, including: children's characteristics; their background and home life; motivation; self-esteem; prior level of learning; the learning environment; the teacher's characteristics; the teacher's experience and attitude to teaching.

Children already *know* lots of music from their background – their enculturation; what they've learnt from the world around them informally. School brings formal instruction, which interacts with their informal enculturation. Successful musical learning will be a combination of the two: learning through active, authentic music-making that children can relate to.

Top tip

In order to deliver authentic, musical activities with a depth of musical knowledge and skills, be sure to cover all three knowledge types in your teaching, keeping the experience of music (knowledge 'of') at the centre.

Musical pedagogy identifies three inter-related types of musical knowledge:

○ **Knowledge 'about'**: the facts, information, the theory of music.

○ **Knowing 'how'**: know-how, practical skills.

○ **Knowledge 'of'**: your relationship with music as a performer, listener or composer/improviser; your *experience* of music.

Let's apply this to learning a well-known song, *We will Rock You* by Queen.

● **Knowledge about:** Queen was a rock group that rose to fame in the 1970s and 1980s. The lead singer was Freddie Mercury. *We will Rock You* was written by guitarist, Brian May, in 1977. The song has four beats in a bar. It has a very simple structure: verse/chorus three times followed by a guitar solo. It is accompanied by rhythm only; it uses no melodic or chordal instruments (until the guitar solo). It has the same rhythm pattern throughout, using stamps and claps.

● **Know-how:** We can count four beats in a bar along with the song. We understand how to stamp/clap the rhythm pattern on the right beats of the bar. It is in the key of E minor and we can play some notes from the scale. We know how to play the chorus using the notes G F♯ E D EE. We know how to sing the verse. We know how to play the chorus.

● **Knowledge of:** We know the song really, really well. We know what it feels like to perform the stamp-stamp-clap rhythm in time with the beat. We can sing the verse with feeling, like a lead singer. We can play the chorus in the right style – as though we are in a rock band. We can improvise using the notes from the chorus. After performing this song, we can pretend to be members of a world famous rock band like Queen. We could compose our own music in this style.

With their enculturation and prior knowledge, children could probably achieve a performance of this song fairly easily; they may already know the song and be familiar with rock music. They could learn to sing/play the song without analysing the 'about' or 'how' content. But together, all three knowledge types underpin the musical knowledge and skills that are needed to know the song really well, and then to be able to apply that learning to another piece of music.

Bonus idea

Think back to a learning experience of your own, e.g. learning your instrument; learning to drive or speak a language. What was the experience like? Can you remember the changes that took place? Do you feel you have knowledge 'of' the subject?

17 Cross-curricular links

"How can I make links with other subjects?"

Making links between music and other subjects integrates music into school life, making it part of the everyday experience. It will also endear you to the class teacher and senior leadership, raising your profile and the position of music in school!

Music is a relatively small part of children's learning; while at school they are immersed in topics, experiences and National Curriculum subjects. English, mathematics and science are the core subjects; music is a foundation subject that jostles for timetable space amongst history, geography, PE and the rest!

Anecdote

Music and the arts can struggle against English and the mighty STEM subjects (Science, Technology, Engineering, Mathematics). However, instrumental learning has many benefits: improved physical coordination, teamwork, listening, patience, technical skills, memory and language skills, confidence, self-esteem, and social/emotional development. Turn STEM into 'STEAM' by adding 'Arts', and music will be integrated and valued throughout the school.

Make links: ask your class what book they are reading in literacy or what they are learning in science or history. Basing improvisation ideas around characters from a book, making up a soundscape about outer space or composing a march for Roman soldiers can produce lesson content which is creative and relevant. (For more topic-based ideas, see Idea 18.)

Links to core subjects

⦿ English: Listen to music and ask children to describe what they hear – encourage descriptive use of language. Use imagination to explore ideas and story-telling through the instrument.

⦿ Mathematics: Count beats and explore time signatures. Work out the subdivisions of the beat mathematically as well as musically. Look for patterns in music, e.g. repeated phrases/rhythm patterns, sequences…

⦿ Science: Understanding how instruments work will support children's playing know-how, as well as supporting their learning of the science National Curriculum (see Idea 19), in which they are asked to: identify how sounds are made and where the vibration comes from; find patterns between pitch and sound production and between the volume of a sound and the strength of vibrations.

Making links to topics

"Let's explore the music of the rainforest!"

KS2 topics are cross-curricular and cover subjects from the Victorians to the environment, offering the opportunity for creative music-making in a variety of genres and styles.

Topics offer the chance to incorporate all kinds of music. Find out what topics your classes are covering and build in those cross-curricular links (see Idea 17). Here are some ideas:

○ **Victorians:** Teach a music hall song.

○ **Stone Age:** Discuss how people may have made music then.

○ **Romans:** Compose a soldiers' march.

○ **Around the World:** Learn a folk tune, a blues or a Bhangra tune.

○ **Festivals and celebrations:** Learn a song to celebrate harvest time, or for Diwali – the Hindu festival of light.

Example: Discover the rainforest

○ **Listening:** Listen to music from a rainforest country (e.g. Colombia, parts of Africa, Brazil…). Discuss what instruments the children hear and how it makes them feel. Explore the similarities and differences with other music the children are familiar with.

○ **Soundscape**: Gather some percussion instruments with a variety of sounds. Discuss how to create the sound of bird song, insects buzzing, frogs croaking, monkey calls, trickling streams, thundering waterfalls, rain and more.

○ **Conduct a rainstorm:** Build the storm by gradually inviting more children to join in/ change action: start by rubbing hands; move to clicking fingers slowly then faster; slap thighs as the storm increases; add thunder claps by all jumping together. Gradually reverse the actions as the storm recedes. Try it on instruments – it is a great way to explore texture.

○ **Word rhythms:** Brainstorm rainforest words and turn them into rhythm patterns to chant, perform on body percussion and then on instruments. Layer the patterns to create a piece of music.

Top tip

Apply the inter-related dimensions (see Idea 8) to your creative music to add variety. Above all, be imaginative and have fun!

19 Instrument investigation

"Miss, what does this do?"

Understanding how instruments work is useful, scientific and can make learning technique more relevant – yes, pressing your finger down hard on the guitar string or completely covering the hole on a woodwind instrument is important because...

Sound is a topic in the science programme of study for Year 4, so it serves a useful cross-curricular purpose to think about sound production and how instruments work (see Idea 17).

○ **What is sound?** When something makes a sound it vibrates, which makes the air around it vibrate. Demonstrate this by plucking a string on a stringed instrument or striking a cymbal or triangle – the instrument only resonates if it is left to 'ring'. Strike a tuning fork and dip it into a bowl of water, the vibration makes the water ripple.

○ **How do we hear sound?** Sound waves enter the outer ear and travel through the ear canal to the eardrum. The eardrum vibrates and sends vibrations via the middle ear to the cochlea in the inner ear. An electrical signal is carried to the brain, which turns it into a sound that we recognise and understand. The musical word for the quality of that sound is 'timbre'.

○ **Categorisation**: Instruments are usually categorised by their four orchestral families: strings, woodwind, brass and percussion. The Hornbostel–Sachs system classifies instruments more scientifically, depending on how the sound is produced, allowing for the inclusion of non-Western instruments:

- **Aerophones**: vibrating columns of air (woodwind/brass instruments).
- **Chordophones**: vibrating stretched string(s) (ukulele, piano, violin, harp).
- **Membranophones**: vibrating stretched skin (all kinds of drums or the kazoo).
- **Idiophones**: the body of the instrument is vibrating (untuned percussion, xylophones).

Taking it further...

Demonstrate instruments and discuss their playing techniques and classification:
- Which orchestral family or H–S classification does each instrument belong to and why?
- How is the sound produced?
- Where is the vibration created?

Bonus idea

Watch a video online of a tuning fork being dipped in water in slow motion, e.g. **tinyurl.com/ y87uz58k**

Warm-ups

"A mental and physical warm-up can concentrate the mind and get every lesson off to a good start."

Do you have a warm-up routine as part of your instrumental practice? As musicians, we know the value of maintaining the body. Physical warm-ups stimulate the blood flow to music-making muscles and focus the mind for learning.

○ Make warm-ups relevant to the main activity of the lesson. If you are learning a tune or a groove with a certain rhythm or a new note, then build a warm-up around it – this makes your lesson content more integrated and saves time later on.

○ Warm up with stretches before playing; shaking out arms and rubbing hands together helps to concentrate the mind and can be fun if done together – make sure children watch for the stop signal! Another stretch and a shake-down after a playing session will relieve aching shoulders or sore hands/fingers.

○ For woodwind and brass players, do some focused breathing exercises followed by long notes or buzzing on the mouthpiece.

○ Copy-backs are a great way to start, combining group playing, note revision, fingering, rhythm patterns, technique and inspirational modelling from you. Rhythms can be as simple or as syncopated as you like, as children are copying what they hear.

'Don't clap this one back'

Clap some four-beat rhythms. When you clap the rhythm, 'Don't clap this one back', children must not clap it back, instead they should put their hands in the air; if they copy it they are out!

ta	ta	te - te	ta
Don't	clap	this one	back

Start with simple rhythms and progress to more syncopated patterns.

Variations: Use different body percussion sounds (timbres). Add different rhythms, e.g. 'Put your hands on your head'.

> **Top tip**
>
> Always maintain good posture. This should be established from the beginning with reminders throughout lessons: sit up straight, sit forward on your chair, feet on the floor please, no crossed legs. Make sure you model good posture when you play.

21 Singing

"A child who plays an instrument before he sings may remain unmusical for a lifetime." (Kodály)

Starting lessons with a song gets music-making happening immediately. Keep singing as an integral part of your lessons both as support for the development of instrumental skills and for its own sake.

Singing in instrumental lessons helps to internalise skills such as pulse and pitch. Sing often and learn a wide range of songs, making sure you choose those with the right range for young voices: a range of around an octave from middle C or just below. Also, use the voice to learn melodies and rhythms before transferring them onto instruments.

Top tip

When you start a song off, set the pitch and tempo with your voice: sing 'ready, off we go' on the starting note with a clear pulse. Encourage children to take turns at being singing leaders.

Taking it further...

See if the school has any song sources you can tap into, e.g. they may have subscribed to *Sing Up* or *Music Express* – these websites have hundreds of songs with backing tracks and teaching ideas. Ask class teachers if they can practise songs with their class between your sessions!

Warming up the voice can be fun and is important. Try these vocal warm-ups:

○ Start with a yawn to open up the throat.

○ Try a tongue twister to warm up the face muscles – chant it on different pitches and at different volumes and tempi.

○ Use different vocal timbres – sing like a robot, the Queen (posh voice), a cowboy, a giant, a mouse...

○ Imagine you are chewing a large toffee – move it around your mouth with your tongue and get all your muscles moving.

○ Make a big (scary) face – open your mouth, eyes and hands WIDE!

○ Make a small face, screw it up tight.

○ Take a relaxed deep breath and sing 'ah' (any pitch) until your breath has run out.

○ Copy back syllables to get the lips and tongue moving: ta ta ta, ka ka ka, ma ma ma, da da da.

○ Sing the word 'sing', holding the 'ng' sound while you swoop up in pitch. Try starting on different pitches; conduct the rate of pitch change with your hands.

Learning by ear

"Learning to play by ear leads to musical fluency — just as learning to talk enables us to engage in conversation."

Aural skills develop musicianship, giving immediate musical results without the hurdle of notation.

In many cultures, music is learned aurally through listening, and passed on orally, without being notated. Nurturing aural skills from the beginning develops children's inner ear and prepares them for playing all styles of music, and potentially, for aural tests in instrumental grade exams.

Learning by ear is an 'informal' learning style – like listening to music with friends and working out the tune, or finding a pop song online and picking out the rhythm pattern or chords. It is a musical life skill that needs to be developed and practised in order to come easily.

● **Copying back phrases:** Warming up with copy-backs is a great way to establish aural learning as a norm in lessons. Starting simply and gradually moving to longer and more complex phrases improves musical memory and children's confidence on their instrument.

● **Listening:** Hone listening skills by listening to music – live or recorded and from a variety of genres. Test children on what they can hear, e.g. which instruments are playing, do the dynamics change? Encourage the children to respond to music through movement. Discuss what features in the music led to them moving the way they did.

● **Spot the difference:** Play a short melody twice, making changes the second time; get children to identify a change to the rhythm, pitch, dynamics, articulation or dynamics.

Anecdote

Indian classical music is based on the 'Guru' model, where a student learns from a master player over a number of years. Similarly, in West Africa, 'Griots' are born into a family tradition passing songs, stories and instrumental mastery down the generations. Jazz and folk are both aural traditions – the main tune in jazz is called the 'head' because it is kept in the head – it might not be written down!

23 Choosing repertoire

"What shall we play?"

Repertoire forms the core of your teaching, so it is important to use music that will engage and stretch your class.

There is little specific WCET repertoire available commercially. Many teachers make up their own music and some hubs have commissioned repertoire. Whatever you use will have an impact on children's engagement and progress. Remember that learning an instrument should be fun! If children are enjoying their lessons, they are more likely to want to learn and try hard.

○ Widen their horizons: Children love to play music they recognise, but it isn't always easy (or appropriate) to play the latest pop song. Widen children's outlook by introducing them to new sounds, styles and genres of music; if repertoire is fun, playable and sounds good, children usually don't mind what they play.

○ Right level: For melodic instruments, choose repertoire that uses the right range of notes for your class.

○ Backing tracks: Backing tracks can make the simplest tune sound interesting and can inspire improvisation and copy-backs too.

○ Simple and repetitive: Choose repertoire with a simple structure and repeated sections so that it is easy to learn aurally. Learning a new piece by ear is the most direct way to get your group improving instrumental skills and it follows on naturally from copy-back activities. Challenge children's listening skills – get them to recognise structures and patterns by watching you playing.

○ Create repertoire: Children love playing their own music to each other; encourage creativity by making up simple riffs and musical ideas that can be extended (see Idea 28).

○ Easily adapted: Differentiate parts so that everyone is challenged – create an 'ostinato' or simplify melodies/harmonies (see Idea 12).

Taking it further...

Try these publications for inspiration:
The Rough Guide to World Music.
Songlines magazine – news and features on world music.
The *English Folk Dance and Song Society* publishes the oldest folk music and dance magazine in the world!
Jazzwise magazine – a guide to jazz in the UK and beyond.
Classical 100 – an online collection of 100 pieces of classical music with information about composers and the story behind the music.

Teaching music musically

"I'm teaching music, of course it's musical!"

You may think this is a no-brainer – that teaching music makes it musical. But is it? Are children actively engaged in authentic music-making? Are they making progress through a broad range of musical activities?

Here are some ideas to keep your music teaching musical!

○ **Start with music:** Avoid unnecessary talking. Sing as you walk to your teaching space or take the register as a musical activity – playing back names as a rhythm or melody (see Idea 4).

○ **Internalise:** Learn new repertoire through singing/chanting and internalising through body movements or body percussion first. When learning pitch, raise/lower your hand for higher/lower notes – get children to do it with you or respond while you are playing.

○ **Teach one idea using a range of approaches:** When teaching a melody, children tap the pulse while you play (tap a different part of the body for each phrase); children sing the note names while you play the tune; all sing the note names and put down the appropriate fingering without playing; half the group play and half sing.

○ **Explore music through listening:** Break phrases down and ask questions – what note/pattern does it start on? Did the next note go up or down in pitch? Was the next pattern the same or different?

○ **Consolidate understanding through playing and modelling**: Ensure you are giving the experience 'of' music, not just learning 'about' music or 'know-how' (see Idea 16).

○ **Get children's attention through music:** The worst thing you can do is shout – this will strain your voice and will not have the desired result of a peaceful, respectful classroom. Do some actions – tap your shoulders/head to a steady beat and eventually the whole class will be following you. Move between the actions quickly to try to catch them out; end by folding your arms.

Taking it further...

Keith Swanwick's book *Teaching Music Musically* (Routledge, 1999) delves deeply into this subject, outlining key principles for musical teaching. It includes ideas on the nature of music itself, its value and metaphorical significance and the social context of musical understanding.

25 Inspiring creativity

"I like making up my own rhythms."

Creativity should be at the heart of your lessons and starts from having the confidence to make musical choices; once children understand what those choices can be, creativity will flow.

Progress may feel slow in WCET – children may be unable to practise and may learn to play just a few notes during the course of a year of lessons. What can be done with just a few notes or sounds? The answer is – anything! We can be creative as soon as we can make a sound.

Word rhythms

Use word rhythms such as the children's names or favourite foods as a springboard for improvising rhythmic or melodic patterns. Start by chanting the word rhythms over a pulse and then transfer to instruments – make sure it is rhythmic and interesting! By inventing their own word rhythms, children are making creative choices and being musical. Using familiar words gives them the confidence to make other choices. Use ideas from the inter-related dimensions of music to add interest and variety to the word rhythms (see Idea 8).

> **Top tip**
>
> Encourage the use of creative adjectives and onomatopoeia words; children are used to doing this in literacy so push them to be ambitious.

> **Bonus idea** !
>
> Children are full of ideas. If you get stuck, ask them!

Use a stimulus to inspire musical ideas

It could be a painting or a piece of music, anything… How does the stimulus make you feel? What does it make you think of? Can you make up a storyline? Have a group discussion and write down some key words, and give each word a musical attribute – a dynamic, a pitch, a tempo or timbre.

Split into groups and give each group one of the words and attributes. Using the notes children know, work on developing musical *motifs*. You can decide on some musical rules or leave the parameters open.

Play the motifs to each other and share feedback. Decide on an order and play them one after another as one big piece. Discuss how the piece sounds; encourage children to think critically about what works and what could be improved.

"Remember to keep your cheeks in!"

We are preparing musicians with the potential for instrumental continuation and progression to school or hub ensembles. Make sure technique is an integral part of musical learning, not simply an aim in itself.

Good technique is fundamental, and we can impart its essence through example: if we play well-produced notes with a good posture and a beautiful tone, then that is what children will emulate.

○ Posture: Teach good posture for playing your instrument, e.g. to sit up straight, feet flat on the floor, hold your head up…

○ Holding instruments: Teach the correct way to hold each instrument.

○ Don't let children get tired: Holding and playing instruments for long periods can be tiring, particularly if they are unable to build stamina by practising between lessons. Rest fingers and lips and change position regularly, e.g. if you want them to play standing up, then sit down while you're not playing.

○ Remember to include ensemble technique: Teach children skills for playing as a group, how to follow a leader and perform in front of an audience.

○ When possible, practise away from the instrument: Practise finger patterns on the back of the hand, tongue twisters for tonguing, tapping rhythm patterns on knees, stroke your tummy up and down for strumming patterns – ask your class to come up with some more ideas.

○ Breath control: Use a palm-sized piece of paper – hold your hand upright in front of your face and blow a steady stream of breath to keep the paper on your hand. How long can you keep the paper up? Make sure cheeks aren't puffing out!

Top tip

Remind children to stand/sit up straight; good playing flows from good posture.

Taking it further…

Build on name rhythms (see Idea 4) as a basis for consolidating technique whilst exploring improvisation – playing familiar patterns means children can focus on technique and good posture. Try repeating this idea with other word rhythms, e.g. favourite football teams – ask the children for ideas and be creative!

27 Improvising

"Let's make something up!"

Improvising is a great way to get playing, and you really don't have to be an expert. In some genres, such as Indian classical music and jazz, improvisation is innate, but if that isn't your background don't panic – just have a go! Take a melody or rhythm and change it – that's improvising.

Adults are more likely to be nervous about improvising than children – if you feel unconfident about making something up, don't pass that nervousness on to the children. Normalise improvisation by including it from the first lesson.

◉ **Copying**: Begin copy-backs by clapping, then move to other body percussion – be creative with different body and vocal sounds. Then move on to instruments. For melodic instruments, start on one pitch first, expanding the range as musical knowledge and technique improves.

◉ **Question and answer**: Once children are confident with copy-backs they can make up their own reply; the answer can have elements of the question in it, which helps those who might not know where to start. Make sure the children know that in this activity the music room is a safe space – there are no 'wrong' notes or rhythms when improvising. Encourage trial and error.

◉ **Scales**: The minor pentatonic (e.g. D F G A C) is a great scale for improvising. Find the best key for your instrument and use notes from this scale for question and answer games.

◉ **Free improvisation**: Have a jam session: free improvisation where 'anything goes'. Decide on a start/stop signal and through gestures only, signal to children to play freely – anything they like. Use dynamics to add drama – try changing suddenly/gradually. Invite volunteers to be the conductor. Try more than one conductor at a time – how does that sound?

Taking it further...

Music examination boards are a great source of ideas and advice on improvising: **trinitycollege.com** has the option to improvise from a motivic, stylistic or harmonic stimulus. **trinityrock.com** includes improvisation in its session skills. **rslawards.com/rockschool** includes improvisation and interpretation. **gb.abrsm.org/en** has jazz exams with backing tracks that can be used to improvise over.

Composing

"Let's make something up and remember it/write it down so that we can play it again!"

Composing is the next logical step from improvising – making something up and then setting it down somehow so that it can be performed again by you or others. There are many ways to start composing; here are two ideas to get you started.

Music for video clips

Watch some short video clips/animations with the sound down, e.g. a cartoon, a rollercoaster, a leopard running across a plain… Discuss what kind of music could go with each clip.

Allocate each clip to a group of children to invent some music. There are no rules. Don't forget the inter-related dimensions – tempo or dynamic changes can be very effective.

Decide how to remember the music – record it, notate it or create a graphic score. Listen to each group playing their composition along with their clip.

What happened next?

Practise using staff notation if children are familiar with it, otherwise use Kodály rhythms or letter names and dots/dashes for note lengths – whatever works best for your children.

In pairs, children invent a simple four-beat rhythm using crotchets and quavers. Melodic instruments then choose up to three notes and turn the pattern into a melody. They play the pattern on their instruments. Do they like the way it sounds? If not, they should make some changes.

Each pair swaps their pattern with another pair. They practise the first pattern and invent a second pattern to make a two-bar phrase. Each pair performs their two-bar phrase to the class.

As a class, choose four phrases and decide what order they should go in to create a longer piece. Give your composition a name and perform it to a teacher or in assembly.

Taking it further...

What tempo should it be? Should it be smooth (*legato*) or spikey (*staccato*)? What style should it be – a dance, spooky, hectic, calm? Can you add words to turn it into a song?

29 Being a conductor

"3, 2, 1, go!"

Anyone can lead an ensemble, right? You just count it in and off we go... or do we? Following a leader or being the conductor takes practice and develops leadership skills alongside learning how to pay attention and being ready to play – looking and listening.

Large ensembles need a conductor to keep performers together, but all groups have a musical leader, someone who starts and stops the music. Communication is their most important asset; a leader uses their body and facial expression to keep time, but also to control the emotion and character of the music – whether they are standing in front with a baton or are part of the ensemble.

With the children, explore different ways to lead your group, and discuss what works best – verbal cues, gestures or traditional conducting patterns; are there other ways? Watch a range of leaders from different genres and discuss how they control the ensemble and what gestures are used; be sure to choose people from a variety of genders and backgrounds.

○ **Visual or audible cues:** Conductors use visual cues; in pop or jazz bands there may be an audible count-in.

○ **Watch choirs from around the world:** The Bulgarian choir *Le Mystère des Voix Bulgares* have a unique sound and sing without a conductor.

> **Anecdote**
>
> Since hearing children start music by saying, "3, 2, 1, go!", I have banned that phrase from the classroom. Instead, I explain the convention of counting in – how to think of the pulse, make eye contact and count, in time upwards, not backwards!

○ **Check out some famous jazz musicians:** American Big Band leaders from the 'swing era' include Duke Ellington and Count Basie, who both led from the piano; contemporary jazz leaders include Carla Bley and Bob Mintzer. UK band leaders include Gary Crosby and YolanDa Brown.

○ **Watch famous orchestral conductors:** Many have a flamboyant style – borrow some of their gestures and take turns to conduct your class orchestra. Watch superstars like Sir Simon Rattle, Gustavo Dudamel, or Mirga Gražinytė-Tyla.

Classroom instruments

"Will I get a different response from my group if we play different instruments?"

Hopefully your school will have a selection of tuned and untuned percussion that you can use. Utilise them to bring variety to your musical activities. Be sure to ask if you can borrow instruments and check if there is a school policy re sharing equipment.

Percussion instruments are easy to hold and play and can bring an immediacy to music-making that is sometimes elusive. Getting away from WCET instruments for a while can be liberating and allow for some fun 'musicking' without a need for techniques that feel complicated or restrictive, whilst still developing ensemble and musicianship skills. Discuss the best way to hold and play the instruments.

○ Create an atmospheric musical soundscape: Use the instruments to create an atmosphere or mood, e.g. how it feels to be in space; a summer's day; dinosaurs having a party! Explore dynamics, tempo, texture etc.

○ Create and layer rhythm patterns: Practise layering the patterns in time to a pulse.

Taking it further...

Put the soundscape and rhythm patterns together to create a piece with two sections. Or, combine your classroom percussion ideas with ideas on your WCET instruments. Create a graphic score or a 'when to play' timeline and give your piece a title. Perform it in assembly or as part of a WCET concert.

1	2	3	4
● Tam　-	● bour　-	● ine	**X** (sh)
○ Tri	-	● an　-	● gle
●　　● Tap　the	● claves,	●　　● tap　the	● claves
● ● ● ● Play ma-ra- cas	●　　● shake shake,	● ● ● ● Play ma-ra- cas	●　　● shake shake

31 Ensemble skills

"I love performing in a group, it makes me feel proud!"

As musicians we know how rewarding it feels to make music with others. WCET is all about playing in groups, so hone those ensemble skills to make playing and performing an enjoyable and satisfying experience.

Playing together can increase confidence and self-esteem and be exciting, releasing endorphins that boost happiness and relieve stress. Developing ensemble skills with your WCET classes will also prepare children to progress to playing in school or hub ensembles.

● Teamwork and collaboration: Let children take the lead – they might choose what to play, decide on the tempo, suggest dynamics, help with decisions on how to start or finish, count in or be the conductor. By taking the lead, they have ownership of the music and will take pride in performing it.

● Rehearsing: It's important that children understand what rehearsing is and how to do it efficiently. Work out the best way to play the piece – if it is long and children get tired, split it into sections and take turns. If you have children who are confident, then designate them as leaders or soloists.

> ### Top tip
>
> Know the pieces thoroughly so that you can make quick alterations to parts or provide additional differentiation where necessary. You will soon become experienced at arranging and adapting 'on the hoof' and will build up a repertoire of pieces that work well.

● Critical thinking: Practise a piece together, then ask the children how they think it sounds and how it could be improved – encourage their critical thinking as well as communicating appropriate praise and sharing your own notes on how to make it better. The National Curriculum for KS2 music says children should *"perform, listen to, review and evaluate music"*. If children understand what good music-making sounds like and how to listen critically, they can make suggestions on how to improve.

● Performing: Make sure children are confident with their parts so there is no physical tension due to nervousness or worry (see Idea 33). Remind children to perform with a good posture and hold instruments correctly, and to smile!

Musical connections

"I remember this pattern — we've played it before!"

Whatever the focus of your lessons, make connections with musical and other aspects of children's learning, from the inter-related dimensions, children's prior learning in WCET and curriculum music lessons, to maths, literacy and classroom topics.

Learning occurs through making connections. Educator Paul Harris calls this 'simultaneous learning'. Think of a piece you are learning, what connections can you make?

○ What do children recognise from other pieces? E.g. rhythms, scalic patterns, chords or fingering.

○ What ideas can you develop? E.g. internalise a pattern or phrase then build on it through improvisation or composition.

○ How can you link with topics? Add topical word phrases to rhythm patterns; explore that further through composition. (See Ideas 17 and 18.)

○ What aspects of technique can you explore? E.g. how to use the breath to control a crescendo.

○ How can you develop general musicianship? E.g. explore singing and internalising rhythms/melodies before playing them, perform to an audience, learn to play from notation…

○ How can you develop children's aural and listening skills? E.g. learning by ear, playing copy-backs that use familiar notes/patterns, focusing on ensemble skills/playing together as a group.

Neuroscientists have observed that brain activity increases when playing an instrument. Language and mathematical skills are controlled by the left hemisphere and creative skills are controlled by the right, and when playing an instrument both sides of the brain are engaged. This can increase memory skills and make musicians better at problem-solving and multi-tasking, leading to the theory that 'music makes you smarter'!

Top tip

Challenge children to listen out for musical connections when learning new repertoire – where have we heard this phrase before? Does the next note go up or down in pitch? Which rhythm/strumming pattern would go well with this tune?

33 Performing

"Celebrating achievement through public events will make young musicians feel proud."

Performing to an audience is an integral part of being a musician; be sure to practise performance skills alongside all those other practical essentials.

Participation in authentic musical experiences practises communication skills, self-expression and interpretation and gives children a sense of accomplishment; it also raises the profile of music and instrumental learning at school.

Checklist ✔

- Showcase repertoire from different styles and genres.
- Include group compositions and improvisation.
- Decide whether to perform from memory or to use visual support.
- Video the performance – check that you have the necessary permissions for each child if you want to make it public.

Top tip

Perform often.
Invite parents.
Wrong notes don't matter – KEEP GOING!
Don't forget to breathe!

⊙ Performing at school: Play in assembly – your group may only know three notes, but make those three notes matter! Establish regular end-of-year performances for parents and invite the year group that will be learning WCET next – they will be inspired at what can be achieved in a year or even a term. Encourage children to help plan and introduce the performance; pride in their achievements will rub off on parents too.

⊙ Other performance opportunities: One of the roles of music hubs is to *"provide opportunities to play in ensembles and to perform from an early stage"* (National Plan for Music Education). Find out what those opportunities are. Playing outside of school and making links with hub ensembles widens children's musical outlook and can inspire them to continue learning their instrument once the WCET programme is over.

⊙ Good preparation will help to avoid performance anxiety: Make sure there is time to warm up physically and mentally. Make sure performers are focused, and play/sing with good posture. Practise mindfulness techniques such as visualisation: before the performance, imagine playing well. If you are using backing tracks make sure the technology is working and that the track is loud enough!

Classroom management

"Two house points for working hard today!"

Managing your group is key to successful music-making. Children respond to clear guidelines and if they are fully engaged in learning, they are less likely to be disruptive.

Teaching WCET is different to one-to-one or small-group teaching, and classroom management may be completely new to you. In general, disruptive behaviour results from being bored, so rule number one is to keep your group engaged. What are you teaching them? How are you teaching it? Do they look interested? Are they all taking part? Is the task pitched at the right level?

If the answer is no, then consider your approach to planning (see Idea 9), your lesson content and repertoire selection (see Idea 23), and differentiation (see Idea 12).

Read your school or hub's behaviour management policy; this is a really good place to start and means your rewards and sanctions will be in line with what the children are used to.

Do you have a teacher or teaching assistant (TA) with you? Could you have?

Develop your own teaching style; set boundaries, be clear, be enthusiastic, use child-friendly language. Most importantly, praise good behaviour rather than pointing out bad behaviour: rewarding good work is more effective than telling children off. Don't only praise good results – give rewards for effort and hard work, not just achievement.

If certain children are being disruptive, speak to the class teacher, music co-ordinator or your music hub – don't suffer in silence. The school will have well-rehearsed consequences and will definitely want to facilitate children's learning.

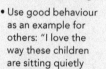

Checklist

- Use good behaviour as an example for others: "I love the way these children are sitting quietly and listening today."
- Model the behaviour you expect from your class.
- Be polite, consistent and fair.
- Use positive language rather than "Don't…"
- Have high expectations.
- Be patient!

Top tip

House points and other similar rewards are quick and easy to give out – but they are valuable, so ration them!

35 Musical fun and games

"I like to play games to change the pace of my lessons."

Learning an instrument isn't easy, but it should be fun! An enthusiastic, light-hearted approach keeps children motivated and can ease technical challenges. Fun activities and games can help build knowledge and allow skills to sink in without lengthy explanations.

Try the following ideas to add some variety to your lessons.

◗ Quick-fire round: Recap learning from previous weeks in a speedy verbal test; act as if you are host of a quiz show – keep it snappy! Don't let children shout out or dominate – take turns or try multiple choice (hands up for A, B, etc.). E.g. What note(s) do we play with these fingers down? What is this string called? What do we call this part of the instrument? How does the timbre change if I play the string here compared to here?

Taking it further...

Develop some of the rhythm patterns children create in *Fish and chips* on instruments, e.g. practise playing them using two different notes or tones.

Bonus idea

See also the following musical games: *Number game* (see Idea 10); *Don't clap this one back* (see Idea 20).

◗ The magic music pen: Imagine you are holding a pen. Draw a shape in the air and as you do, make a vocal sound that goes with it – a 'whoosh', an 'oooeeeooo' that rises and falls in pitch, the sound of a steam train... You must make a sound otherwise the pen stops working. Pass the pen to your neighbour, they must start immediately with your sound then change it to a new one.

◗ I like fish and chips: Clap or play the pattern of the words: 'I like fish and chips'. The game is to pass the pattern around the class and for each child to change 'fish and chips' to a food they like. Discuss examples first, e.g. 'I like fruit' is easy; 'I like spaghetti hoops' is tricky; 'I like chicken burgers' is more achievable.

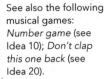

ta	ta	te - te	ta
I	like	fish and	chips

Backing tracks **36**

"Miss, this song is sick! I like the way it helps me know when to play and when to stop."

Backing tracks encourage playing with style and imagination and can make a piece with just one note sound cool! They are easy to find online – a quick search brings up various backings, including karaoke tracks of popular songs – or you could make your own!

Playing with a backing track provides structure, supports authentic music-making and immediately makes beginners both sound and feel better about their playing.

A drum track can support activities around playing in time: clapping the pulse; feeling the first beat of the bar; clapping on a particular beat; taking turns to clap/play patterns over the track; making up new patterns. A good drum track will have fills at the ends of sections which provide cues so that children get a sense of when to play.

Find tracks in different styles and genres, e.g. use notes from the blues scale to play over a bluesy guitar track. A drone track presents a more open palette of options. Look for Arabic grooves, Indian *tanpura* and *tabla*, one-chord jazzy tracks or spacey soundscapes.

Inventing your own

Have a go at making your own backing track; if you have an Apple product you automatically have *GarageBand*. If you've never tried it before, open the app now – it's very intuitive! (There are plenty of video tutorials online if you're not sure where to start.)

You can easily make a drum track by using sampled instrumental loops and have hours of fun with fantastic sounds from around the world. Try these free Digital Audio Workstations (DAWs): *GarageBand, Soundtrap, Audacity, Pro Tools First, Cubase LE, Cakewalk, Ableton Live Lite.*

Taking it further...

Drone backings encourage exploration of new tonalities. Try playing the white notes E–E (Phrygian mode with flattened supertonic). It is called raga 'Bhairavi' in Indian classical music and is used in Spanish flamenco music.

Anecdote

Demi loved the 'sick' dance-anthem feel of my WCET tune *Lay Down the Bass*. I wrote it to practise playing C–F, but the beats and loops on the backing track got feet tapping and inspired some groovy (sitting down) dance moves!

---

37 Zen

"I try to follow the aims of this Japanese school of Buddhism."

If this book was an A–Z, it would end with Zen: be calm and patient in your lessons. The popular meaning of Zen is to feel peaceful and relaxed, relating to mindfulness, or focusing on the moment. This idea is about developing a Zen approach to teaching and learning.

No one said teaching was easy. A class of children can be a daunting sight and there can be many frustrations along the way. We all have bad days, and so do children. Even the weather can affect their mood – if it has been raining, it means wet play, so there will be pent up energy which can lead to disruption. Be prepared to adjust your teaching to accommodate a lively or a downbeat group!

Bonus idea

If children are getting fidgety, try this popular mindfulness technique:
S = Stop what you are doing.
T = Take a deep breath and release it slowly, do this three times.
O = Observe what is happening around you and how you feel inside.
P = Proceed.

Taking it further...

Find out more about mindfulness at **mindfulschools.org**

○ **Establish some routines:** To deliver lessons that go smoothly without frustration, keep things simple, be prepared and have routines. Children like routines. Routine avoids wasting time and removes barriers to learning. If furniture needs to be moved to prepare the room, then establish a structured weekly process – no discussion, everyone will soon get used to it.

○ **Don't stress over things you can't change:** Change what is within your power, use your energy creatively, not negatively. If you are struggling with an aspect of your teaching, then talk to the class teacher or the music co-ordinator. You may find this opens up dialogue that you haven't had before, giving you a support network. Bear in mind you may not get the desired result; some things just can't be changed…

○ **Mindfulness:** Children may already practise mindfulness in class. It can increase their capacity for focus, concentration, memory and creativity. Training the mind to settle and focus on the moment can also alleviate performance anxiety – don't dwell on the past, ignore mistakes or wrong notes!

"Keep It Simple, Stupid!"

KISS also stands for 'Keep It Short and Simple' and 'Keep It Simple and Straightforward'. The message is clear – streamline your planning and don't over-complicate things.

Keeping something simple enough to follow and maintain makes perfect sense – a straightforward lesson plan might feel boring or even 'stupid' to you, but remember the children are in the early stages of development so information needs to be easy to digest. Applying the KISS principle to your lessons will give children the greatest chance of learning thoroughly with deeper comprehension.

● **Create clear, consistent boundaries:** Have simple 'rules' or guidelines for learning, e.g. "Instruments in rest position while I'm talking"; "Only play when I ask you to".

● **Don't talk too much:** Teach via modelling – children will learn through imitation.

● **Use child-friendly language**: Make sure children understand a word like 'dynamics' before you use it. They will be familiar with the concept of volume, so use both words alongside a musical demonstration and children will soon understand the meaning and application of dynamics.

● **Learn by 'doing':** Active learning comes from a theory by John Dewey, an American philosopher. Make activities practical and inclusive so that everyone can engage in the direct experience of music-making. A process of trial and error, or learning through exploration, results in 'procedural knowledge' – knowledge discovered through practical application, or problem-solving.

Anecdote

I once observed a lesson in which 8-year-olds were introduced to their new instrument, told how to hold it, pluck the strings, hold and use the bow, apply rosin, name the parts of the instrument, name the strings and read (simple) stave notation – all in one lesson with very little music-making! I imagine children took very little away from that session. I would rather they had played something simple together with musicality, enjoyment and understanding.

39 Rhythmic notation

"Sound before symbol..."

There are several ways of writing music down, including staff notation, tab and the graphic score. Some cultures don't write music down at all and much music is played and performed away from 'the dots'. Be sure to introduce notation methods in a practical and musical way, but always remember to teach sound before symbol!

Notation is a tool, and musical literacy should follow on from musical fluency. Without notation much Western classical music wouldn't exist – a symphony would be regarded as being too complicated to learn by ear and too long to remember!

The National Curriculum states that *"pupils should be taught to use and understand staff and other musical notations"*. If you are teaching a melodic instrument, an introduction to staff notation makes sense, and guitar and ukulele players should be aware of tab. Traditionally djembe players don't use notation, but as a learning tool and a memory aid, rhythmic and grid notation can be helpful. Make sure children are comfortable with playing rhythm patterns before introducing any kind of notation: 'sound before symbol'.

Bonus idea !

Ask for volunteers to be 'human notation'. Try using children standing in a row: one child is a crotchet, two with straight arms touching each other's shoulders are quavers, and sitting on a chair is a rest. Ask children to arrange how they are going to stand/sit – by doing this they are composing their own rhythms!

Hand notation

◉ Hold up four fingers, count a pulse and ask your group to clap once for each finger, point to each finger as they play – **make sure everyone is looking at your hand**.

◉ Hold one finger down. Explain that it is still there, but that beat is silent – a rest. Ask children to say 'sh' instead of clapping on that beat. Change the fingers you are holding down so that the rest/s move to different beats.

◉ Join your first and second and your third and fourth fingers together (known as the 'Vulcan salute' in Star Trek!). To create two-beat sounds, clap, and then keeping your hands

together, move your hands forward for the second beat, implying the continuation of sound.

◉ Once children are happy clapping the rhythms, they can read the hand notation on their instrument.

The Kodály method

This is a way of introducing staff notation by speaking syllables:

| ta | te - te | ta-aa | sh |

Kodály rhythm flashcards can be found online, and are a great way to introduce rhythm learning. Try clapping, saying and then playing rhythms like this:

| ta | ta | te - te | ta |

Rhythm grids

Start by asking the children to play/say one line at a time. You can then progress to asking them to play/say all four lines one after the other or in groups at the same time, and even backwards or vertically.

Beats	1	2	3	4
1	ta	sh	te - te	ta
2	ta	te - te	ta	sh
3	te - te	sh	ta -	aa
4	ta	sh	te - te	ta

Adapt the grid for djembe or percussion patterns, e.g. for pattern 1:

	1	2	3	4
Bass	X		X X	
Tone		X		
Slap				X

Taking it further...

Zoltán Kodály was a Hungarian composer, ethnomusicologist and teacher who developed a comprehensive method for teaching music theory to children. Find out more at **kodaly.org.uk**.

40 Pitch notation

"The pitch gets higher as you climb up the ladder."

Once children are familiar with rhythmic notation, introduce the idea of pitch; think of the stave as a pitch ladder.

If you have been indicating pitch with your hands while playing and singing melodies (see Idea 8), then children will be used to the concept of high and low notes. Introduce the stave as a ladder where notes climb higher step by step. Add note heads to Kodály rhythm patterns, or just use a blob, then apply the notes to the ladder. Have some fun getting children to move a note up and down the ladder and sing or play the changes in pitch.

Floor stave

Use masking tape to draw a huge stave on the floor and designate children to organise themselves as notes on the lines and in the spaces. Explore moving higher and lower; can they put themselves in the right places to make a scale? Add rhythm: one child is a crotchet, two with straight arms touching each other's shoulders are quavers, crouching down is a rest. Play the patterns on your instruments.

Adding notes to a blank stave

Draw a blank stave on the board and introduce the notes children have learnt to play so far. Invite children to make up melodies by placing notes on the stave and try playing them on instruments.

Anecdote 💬

Crotchet means 'hook' in French! It looks like a crochet needle with its up-turned end.
A stave (or staff) is a stick, so the musical stave is simply a series of sticks, like a ladder or a fence turned on its side.

Graphic scores

"How shall we draw this sound?"

A visual representation of music using symbols unrelated to traditional notation is a great way to get children composing from a visual starting point.

A graphic score can be as simple as adding note names to a grid, e.g.

	1	2	3	4
1	C	sh	E E	D
2	C	D D	E	sh
3	D D	sh	C	D
4	E	sh	D D	C

Top tip

Ask the class teacher if there is a space to display the graphic scores on the walls at school.

Or, marks in the grid can represent an instrument. Explore this idea on classroom percussion or on your WCET instruments; ask children to draw the pictures and decide when each instrument should play, e.g.

Instrument	1	2	3	4
	X	X X	sh	X
	sh	X X	X X	X X
	X X	X	sh	X
	X X	sh	X X	sh

Taking it further...

Show the children examples of graphic notation online, e.g. the amazing artistic creations from composers of concert music such as György Ligeti, John Cage and Cornelius Cardew.

Patterns can also be free form – wavey shapes, splodges, dots, lines – there are no rules!

Be creative! Make up your own shapes to interpret as a selection of free sounds, to illustrate one of the inter-related dimensions or as a soundscape to accompany a storyline.

42 Keep it real!

"I like to include real music in my lessons and play it with style."

Children have access to recorded music as never before – they know what 'real' music sounds like. Teaching music that sounds real makes links to children's life outside the classroom and embeds authentic music-making in their lives.

The classroom can be an artificial place, but making connections to real life helps children relate to instrumental learning as a life choice, not just something they do at school. Children love to play music they know – choose carefully and mix repertoire up by introducing new styles. Keep the experience 'authentic' by introducing children to genres connected with the instrument they are learning.

○ **Demonstrate authentic styles on your instrument:** Play genres stylistically. Show examples of your instrument in real music situations and showcase a variety of genres and cultures. Tell them about your experience as a musician.

○ **Relate instrumental learning to real-life music:** The djembe is from West Africa so incorporate songs and rhythms from the region; if you're learning Queen's *We will Rock You*, play it with rockstar attitude! Compose and improvise in real styles: make up a chorus for a pop song or a jazzy tune using notes from the blues scale and syncopated rhythms.

○ **Ask children what songs they want to learn:** If you think their suggestion is musically unsuitable, explain why so that their next choice can be more informed (if you don't know the song, look it up!).

Top tip

Teach to your strengths. If you feel you are weak in an area, then find out more – watch other teachers, attend CPD or read up on the subject.

○ **Pop songs with easy chord progressions and pentatonic tunes work well:** Playing the melody using just a few notes may not sound like the original, so as a group, think of creative ways to play a simplified version. Play along with the original, working on style and rhythmic accuracy. Encourage children to listen at home and work out how to play the next bit.

"I believe that the school must represent present life – life as real and vital to the child as that which he carries on in the home, in the neighborhood, or on the playground."
(John Dewey)

Collaboration

"You are not alone!"

As musicians we are used to collaborating when we perform or rehearse with others, but being a visiting music teacher can sometimes feel lonely. In the spirit of collaboration, broaden your network by connecting with colleagues at school.

Sharing of specialists' musical skills and class teachers' expertise in classroom management can be invaluable in supporting smooth and musical music lessons. In reality, timetables and budgets may make it impossible for the class teacher to join in, but if possible encourage them to have a go, even if it's not every week. Children love to see their teachers learning alongside them, and will also see that adults may struggle, but make progress.

Collaborating with teachers and TAs can enrich your teaching. They are experts in pedagogy and classroom management and they know the children. They model good behaviour and can address any issues.

Make sure you start building your relationships from the beginning:

● Discuss practical routines for the beginning and end of each session – if you are going to be moving furniture, it is best to check it's okay with the classroom teacher first!

● Share your goals with the class teacher – children will make more progress if the class teacher is promoting the sessions and actively encouraging children to practise.

● Find out about any children with SEND and work together to consider suitable strategies for offering the best support (see Idea 44).

● If possible, meet with the music co-ordinator at the beginning of the year to discuss common goals.

● Arrange performance dates and get them in the school diary.

● Find out about in-school progression routes, e.g. band, drum club, orchestra or choir.

> **Top tip**
>
> Collaboration can bring about a closer working relationship with school-based staff and a common understanding. This will help you to manage your aspirations and expectations and lead to successful musical learning. So, speak to the teachers, find the staffroom and become part of the school community.

44 Being inclusive

"Miss, I can't do it..."

WCET is aimed at the whole class, regardless of their musical ability, background (social and musical), physical ability or special needs. Being inclusive means equality of access – giving everyone the opportunity and space to succeed and reach their potential.

Children have diverse needs and are all entitled to a rich music education. High expectations should apply to your whole group and it's up to you to differentiate your approach to meet all needs. This isn't always easy! Speak to the class teacher about strategies for ensuring that every child has the opportunity to flourish and contribute to music-making with a sense of achievement.

Every mainstream school has a SENCO (SEND co-ordinator); they can offer advice about inclusive approaches. Children with SEND will often have a teaching assistant to support them; they can also help you to find the best way for a child to take part. Consider ways to adapt instruments so they are easier to hold, use smaller chairs/instruments, give ear defenders to those who struggle with loud noises, discuss agreements for children to have time out if needed.

SEND conditions include:

- Emotional and behavioural difficulties (EBD) – low self-esteem/confidence, difficulty following rules, settling down or behaving.
- Autism (including Asperger's syndrome) – affects communication and social interaction.
- Attention deficit (hyperactivity) disorder (ADHD/ADD) – inattentiveness, hyperactivity and impulsiveness.
- Specific learning difficulties, e.g. dyslexia.
- Communication difficulties – difficulty in expressing themselves or understanding what others are saying, making friends or relating to others.
- Medical needs, including epilepsy, mobility difficulties, allergies and visual or hearing impairment.

Taking it further...

These websites offer a starting point for further investigation into SEND and how additional needs can be supported at school:
drakemusic.org,
nhs.uk,
autism-society.org,
gov.uk/children-with-special-educational-needs

Practice and motivation

"Learning how to practise helps us learn how to improve."

Your group may or may not be able to take instruments home to practise regularly, so how do you maintain motivation and inspire children to practise?

This is the million-dollar question! Here are some ideas to help with motivation.

○ Promote children's choice and ownership: Children may not have been able to choose their WCET instrument, so give them agency regarding musical decisions such as repertoire, tempo/dynamics, counting in, conducting or playing a solo.

○ Give appropriate praise: Don't say everything sounds brilliant, it probably doesn't, but it should sound better than last time it was played. Be positive in your feedback, including ideas on how to improve. If children feel they are succeeding, their confidence, enjoyment and commitment will grow and they are more likely to continue playing (see Idea 5).

○ Teach children how to practise: This is an important skill. Make time for it in lessons and teach good practice habits, e.g. demonstrate how to break down a tune or rhythm pattern into chunks and work on it slowly – understanding *how* to improve can make practice less of a chore and more rewarding.

○ Organise a performance: Working towards a concert or assembly performance can inspire practice and gives real meaning to the concept of working at something until it sounds good (see Idea 33).

If children can't take instruments home, ask the class teacher or music co-ordinator if they can organise a practice club or time for them to practise at lunchtime or after school. If children can practise at home, it is crucial to get parents/carers on board; make them aware of how important their support is and get them along to school performances so that children understand the context of their child's instrumental learning (see Idea 47).

> **Bonus idea** !
>
> If your school or music hub website has a music page, find out if you can upload resources so that children can access them between lessons.

> **Top tip**
>
> Never underestimate the power of rewards for hard work – give out stickers, stars, house points or other school rewards – sparingly!

46 Progression – what next?

"I want to keep on playing."

What routes are there for children to continue to play an instrument after their funded WCET programme has come to an end? Hopefully children will enjoy playing and want to carry on; this idea looks at opportunities and potential hurdles to continuation after WCET.

WCET might be the only opportunity some children get to interact with music-making and, in particular, instrumental learning. After engaging with a rich instrumental programme we want all learners to achieve their musical potential and have the opportunity to carry on. Although continuation isn't the only measure of success, a class that promotes enthusiastic, creative music-making underpinned with technical skills and understanding will create musicians ready to move on and play with others.

The following factors can influence whether a child continues with instrumental learning after WCET.

○ **The school culture:** Is music valued and promoted? Are instrumental lessons available to follow WCET? Is there a band or orchestra? Are there regular performance opportunities? Are there links with the music hub? If not, be pro-active and see what you can do to turn the culture around.

○ **Parental attitudes**: If parents are aware of their children's participation and enjoyment of music, they are more likely to support learning and encourage continuation. Try to get them involved early on (see Idea 47).

○ **Cost:** This may be a barrier for parents – your school will know if this is the case. Find out if lessons can be subsidised through pupil premium, hub subsidies or the opportunity for local or national music scholarships.

Top tip

Progression to small-group teaching after WCET means a change to your pedagogical approach. Instead of learning aurally within the protection of a large group, children will now hear themselves playing individually, may move to reading notation and taking an instrument home to practise. Pave the way for these changes so that children know how to cope with a different style of learning and new expectations.

● **Music hub ensembles:** Ensuring that progression routes are available and affordable is a core music hub role (see Idea 48). Make sure all stakeholders are aware of hub opportunities, such as local music centres.

● **Transition**: Moving from primary to secondary school is a potential stumbling block to continuation. Joining hub ensembles while still at primary school can help to bridge this gap – establishing learning outside of school means that transition need not interrupt instrumental learning.

What can you do to promote continuation?

● Set up small-group continuation instrumental lessons before WCET ends.

● If you can, invite other instrumental teachers who teach at the school to demo their instrument to the class; children may prefer to continue their musical learning on a different instrument – this still counts as musical continuation and is a success!

● If your timetable allows, create an ensemble for those showing talent and/or enthusiasm.

● Signpost children to hub ensembles and opportunities. Many local music centres have beginner groups that take players of WCET level.

● If possible, take your group to perform at hub concerts and events; seeing other children perform promotes awareness of progression pathways, inspires continuation and helps to strengthen links between schools, parents and the music hub.

Anecdote

When I started teaching WCET at one particular school, there was very little music-making there so I started up continuation brass lessons. This led to the establishment of a school band and soon other instrumental tutors were engaged. Music is now thriving, with instrumental learning happening across the school and an excellent band which performs regularly at school and hub events.

47 Parents and carers

"My mum doesn't like me practising at home..."

Parental support, or lack of, can make or break a child's musical start. A supportive parent or carer will ensure that their child has access to all the opportunities school can deliver; a child in a less supportive situation can struggle with access to music and the arts.

Research into WCET shows how important parental support is to a child's instrumental continuation, so it is crucial that your musical activities at school are visible to parents and carers, so that they – and teachers – are aware and see the value of music in the life of children and indeed the whole school. Make the whole community aware of music – give the class teacher information about your sessions for their class page on the school website and get your concerts and progress reports included in the school newsletter.

Top tip

If children are able to take instruments home to practise, do check with the class teacher whether playing in the family environment is possible. Children may be embarrassed if they're not allowed to play at home. See if the school can offer access to a school practice club – even playing for ten minutes a week is better than not at all.

The value parents and carers attach to music will have a big impact on the encouragement they give their children. They don't need to be able to play an instrument themselves, but if they observe children enjoying music, it will be seen as a valuable part of education; after all, WCET may be the only chance many children will have to learn an instrument.

The best way for music to be visible is through performances (see Idea 33). Make sure parents and carers are invited to attend concerts or class performances in assembly. Scheduling concerts at the beginning or end of the day (around the school run) means more parents and carers are likely to be able to come.

"Hubs are there to provide opportunities for joined-up music education provision."

Your hub is a source of support for you and your school/s. It is worth taking advantage of what they offer, whether it is CPD, performance opportunities and progression routes for children or curriculum provision and resources.

Hubs came into existence in England in 2012 after the publication of the *National Plan for Music Education.* They are funded (at least in part) by the Arts Council and their roles at the time of writing are given below. Delivery of WCET is embedded as a core role, as is providing opportunities to play in ensembles and follow the progression routes; the extension roles are there to support its delivery.

Core roles

- *Ensure that every child aged five to 18 has the opportunity to learn a musical instrument (other than voice) through whole-class ensemble teaching programmes for ideally a year (but for a minimum of a term) of weekly tuition on the same instrument.*
- *Provide opportunities to play in ensembles and to perform from an early stage.*
- *Ensure that clear progression routes are available and affordable to all young people.*
- *Develop a singing strategy to ensure that every pupil is singing regularly and that choirs and other vocal ensembles are available in the area.*

Extension roles

- *Offer Continuous Professional Development (CPD) to school staff, particularly in supporting schools to deliver music in the curriculum.*
- *Provide an instrument loan service, with discounts or free provision for those on low incomes.*
- *Provide access to large scale and/or high quality music experiences for pupils, working with professional musicians and/or venues. This may include undertaking work to publicise the opportunities available to schools, parents/carers and students.*

Taking it further...

Find out more by visiting Arts Council England: **artscouncil.org.uk/music-education/music-education-hubs**.

49 Safeguarding

"Stay safe at school and make sure the children in your care are safe."

Safeguarding means protecting children – keeping them safe and preventing them from harm. As well as safeguarding children, be aware of the importance of protecting yourself.

Top tip

You need a disclosure and barring service check (DBS) to work with children. Schools will also ask to see evidence of recent Safeguarding training, so make sure you keep this up-to-date.

Taking it further...

Government documents include: *Keeping children safe in education* and *Guidance on the application of... the General Data Protection Regulation*, see **gov.uk**. The Musicians' Union **musiciansunion. org.uk** and the Incorporated Society of Musicians **ism.org** both have advice about safeguarding and child protection and on protecting yourself.

Be professional whilst at school. You are in a position of trust and you must manage personal boundaries. Dress appropriately, and don't swear or make inappropriate remarks to children, even in fun, as this could be misinterpreted.

Avoid touching children. This can be difficult with instrumental teaching as you may want to move a child's arm or finger position, but physical contact could be misinterpreted – avoid it by demonstrating and modelling instead.

Never have contact on social networking sites or share personal details with a child.

All schools have a designated safeguarding lead (DSL). Make sure you know who this is and that you are familiar with the safeguarding and child protection policy. If you have concerns about your own safety or about a child regarding suspected harm, bullying or abuse, then speak to the DSL immediately – don't discuss issues with the child or anyone else.

Don't ask questions about children's home life; it could cause embarrassment.

GDPR compliance (general data protection regulation) affects the use and storage of personal data. Be careful with documents: registers should be first names only and don't use children's surnames in emails.

Developing your practice 50

"#MusicEducation."

Keeping yourself up-to-date through continuous professional development (CPD) is important in supporting you to maintain and enhance your knowledge and skills, not just for career development, but to keep you interested and interesting!

○ Keep a CPD diary: This is useful for your CV as well as making sure you experience a variety of input.

○ Ask your music hub about training opportunities: Most hubs hold CPD events or an annual education conference.

○ Mentoring scheme: If you are just starting out, ask the music hub if there is a mentoring scheme for new WCET teachers.

○ Watch others: Watch an experienced teacher at work.

○ Be brave, obtain peer feedback: Invite a fellow WCET teacher to observe your lesson and give you feedback.

○ Watch yourself teaching: With the school's permission, set up a video – on yourself, not on the children – and give yourself some feedback!

○ Explore social media: Many teachers and music academics write blogs: subscribe to get great ideas popping into your inbox regularly. Twitter is a great source of information but be selective; educators, music academics, arts organisations and education bodies will provide information, debate and new ideas to follow up.

○ Expand your qualifications: Various options exist, from a PGCE aimed at instrumental teachers to a postgraduate Certificate, Diploma or Master's degree in music education. The Level 4 Certificate for Music Educators is specifically for those who are involved in teaching children, and it enables practitioners to develop new skills and consolidate their understanding of music education.

Taking it further...

These professional organisations provide information on CPD:
Music Mark:
musicmark.org.uk
Incorporated Society of Musicians (ISM):
ism.org
Musicians' Union (MU):
musiciansunion.org.uk
Music Teachers' Association (MTA):
musicteachers.org

Recommended further reading (a selection)

Repertoire and resources

Are You Ready? by Kay Charlton (Warwick Music) – Progressive WCET repertoire with backing tracks

Music Express (Collins Music, 2014) – Primary music curriculum resource

Primary Music Toolkit by Dr Alison Daubney (ISM Trust) – A guide to teaching curriculum music

Books

How to Teach Instrumental and Singing Lessons by Karen Marshall and Penny Stirling (Collins Music, 2017)

Improve Your Teaching! Teaching Beginners: A New Approach for Instrumental and Singing Teachers by Paul Harris (Faber, 2008)

Instrumental Teaching: A Practical Guide to Better Teaching by Susan Hallam (Heinemann, 1998)

Instrumental Teaching by Janet Mills (OUP, 2007)

Simultaneous Learning: The Definitive Guide by Paul Harris (Faber, 2014)

Teaching Music Musically by Keith Swanwick (Routledge, 2011)

The Music Teacher's Companion: A Practical Guide by Paul Harris and Richard Crozier (ABRSM, 2000)

Magazines

Music Teacher **musicteachermagazine.co.uk**

Primary Music Magazine **musiceducationsolutions.co.uk**

Reports/documents

Returning our Ambition for Music Learning: Every Child Taking Music Further (Music Commission) **musiccommission.org.uk**

The National Curriculum for Music: A Revised Framework for Curriculum, Pedagogy and Assessment Across Primary Music by Dr Alison Daubney and Professor Martin Fautley (ISM, 2019) **ism.org**

Whole Class Ensemble Teaching (WCET) Final Report by Susan Hallam (Music Mark, 2016)

Whole Class Ensemble Teaching Research Report by Fautley et al. (Music Mark/Birmingham City University, 2017)